T0106357

HOW TO ALWAYS WIN A FIGHT

DENNIS KIM

iUniverse, Inc.
New York   Bloomington

How to always win a fight

Copyright © 2010 by Dennis Kim

All rights reserved. No part of this book may be used or reproduced by any means, graphic, electronic, or mechanical, including photocopying, recording, taping or by any information storage retrieval system without the written permission of the publisher except in the case of brief quotations embodied in critical articles and reviews.

The views expressed in this work are solely those of the author and do not necessarily reflect the views of the publisher, and the publisher hereby disclaims any responsibility for them.

iUniverse books may be ordered through booksellers or by contacting:

iUniverse
1663 Liberty Drive
Bloomington, IN 47403
www.iuniverse.com
1-800-Authors (1-800-288-4677)

Because of the dynamic nature of the Internet, any Web addresses or links contained in this book may have changed since publication and may no longer be valid.

ISBN: 978-1-4401-2607-9 (sc)
ISBN: 978-1-4401-2606-2 (ebk)

Printed in the United States of America

iUniverse rev. date: 12/29/2009

Preface

This book was written for ordinary people, especially those who are not familiar with fighting such as women and weak people.

The world is developing fast. The development in our civilization makes our life more convenient and somewhat more abundant, but on the other hand, there is a duality where crimes are more common and more spiritual stress is added.

The spiritual stress in modern society is not visible through our external appearance; however, it threatens us as much as physical injuries. In a certain way, we can say that spiritual stress is a more critical enemy because it can even destroy our very existence.

If we talk in general about self-defense, we usually have a fixed idea that it is a technique (physical self-defense) that helps us defend our body when we are attacked. Yet, I have added another technique (mental self-defense), which helps us defend our mind from spiritual stress, to the self-defense techniques.

Physical Self-Defense

I hesitated very much to write this book because many martial artists might blame the techniques in this book. Most of the self-defense techniques here are to introduce how to attack vital parts of human body. Due to the danger that they might cause serious injuries or even death if used wrongly, these techniques are not taught at martial arts gyms. Moreover, modern martial arts prohibit the usage of these techniques as they call them **foul plays**.

Yet, most of these techniques are the secrets of Eastern martial arts that have been used in actual fights. Since most martial arts were born for the need of survival skill in a life or death situation, it might not make any sense to talk about foul play in a real war. After all, the concept of **foul play** does not exist within the original techniques of martial arts.

In dealing with violent crime, sports martial arts have its limits. We need to use all the defense techniques including what modern sports martial arts call "**foul play**" in order to protect our self-respect and our family from violence.

Self-defense techniques taught in the gyms are so complex and difficult that ordinary people cannot use them as freely as they want in a real fighting situation. Even though women can learn self-defense techniques for several years and command them freely, it is almost impossible for them to defeat a molester because of her physical inferiority. Furthermore, people who have no talent or never been trained in martial arts cannot help being defenseless when they confront their enemies.

I have written this book for such underprivileged people. I am sure that anyone can learn the techniques from this book in a short period and these actual self-defense techniques will make us to overcome physical disadvantage in the twinkling of an eye.

Mental Self-Defense

Meditation through Danjeon breathing is one of the self-defense techniques (mental self-defense) that can protect you from spiritual stress. Danjeon breathing is a method that Eastern Buddhists, and martial artists have practiced since long time ago. In fact, many westerners think that meditation through Danjeon breathing is difficult because they perceive it as a special practice for only special people. However, I have here summarized Danjeon breathing so that everyone would be able to learn and use it easily. Also, I have here summarized the techniques for mental self-defense so that everyone can practice it easily by himself.

After learning all these techniques in this book, you will have gained a self-confidence, which means you will not fear anybody whoever might threaten you. However, I do recommend you to use the techniques for attacking vital spots only in a critical situation because they can be fatal to other people.

I want to make very clear here that I am not legally responsible for anything that might happen due to the abuse or wrong application of the techniques. All the legal problems are your responsibility.

What you must know before learning the techniques

These techniques for physical self-defense may cause your opponent to lose his balance in a second as you can defeat him easily by using them. However, I recommend that in case a woman encounters a molester and uses the techniques, she must run away as soon as the molester is out of balance. Keep in mind that the chances for women to be able to beat men are very slim indeed.

This book proceeds as follows:

\<Self-Defense of the body\>
Ⅰ. **Vital spot attack** - It is a strong and fatal technique to attack vital points. This is a technique that you can use in order to win whenever you fight.

Ⅱ. **Self-Defense for life** - These techniques can protect you in the complicated society.

Ⅲ. **Knife attack & defense** - It is how to handle a knife for your life.

\<Self-Defense of the mind\>
Ⅳ. **Danjeon breathing** - It is how to treat the stress related with mental injuries.

Contents

Preface

What you must know before learning the techniques

Physical Self-Defense

I. Vital spot attack

II. Self-Defense techniques in daily life

III. Knife attack & defense

Mental Self-Defense

IV. Danjeon Breathing

Physical Self-Defense

I. Vital spot attack

You can fell a tiger only with your finger – Piercing Eye

There was a boy in a small town, called Dennis. He was small, thin and shy with glasses. Everybody in his class looked down upon him, and one big boy among them always teased and harassed him whenever he saw Dennis. The big guy's name was Junior Dog. Junior Dog tripped him up in the classroom, spat on his food in the dining hall, and even hung him in a locker. Dennis was a victim of bullying, and tried to escape the situation several times.

Dennis was trained in Taekwondo, Boxing, Aikido and so on, but had no talent for these areas. He was nervous and scared to go to school. Only his best friend Honey, an old bald spotted dog, used to console him.

One day Dennis was sitting on a bench with Honey in a park, looking at someone exercising. He always sat on that bench whenever he came to the park but had never seen the man before. The man was a stranger, who looked like an Oriental. His kicks and punches were very fast and powerful. Dennis had ever seen many masters in martial arts gyms, but the man's movements seemed to be a little different. Dennis could feel overflowing power and speed of the man even from far away. After finishing his exercise, the man walked toward Dennis with a smile.

"Good afternoon, I'm from Korea," said the man.
"Hi! I'm Dennis," said Dennis.
"My name is Dennis Kim. We have the same name, Dennis."
"Are you a martial artist? Your movements seem different from any other martial artist," said Dennis.

"Yes, I am Hapkidoist. Hapkido is one of Korea's martial arts," said the man.

"I have trained Taekwondo, boxing and Aikido, but it's very difficult to use the techniques in a real fight. Moreover, I have no talent for them," said Dennis.

"Well... that's interesting!!   Yes, sometimes the techniques of martial arts are useless in a real fight even for me. A very practical fighting technique that you can use well could be the most effective one in a real fight," said the man.

The man continued. "Long time ago, there was a man who trained martial art in a deep mountain. He trained himself for a long time, but had no confidence in his ability to defeat whoever challenges him to fight. One day when he trained on a rock, a big wild tiger jumped in front of him roaring with its mouth wide open. They started to fight. He kicked and punched it, but the tiger seemed not to be hurt at all. He began to be tired and nervous. He jumped and got on the back of the tiger, hugging the tiger's neck. The tiger jumped up and down like crazy in order to make him fall off, and he was getting exhausted. At the very moment when he was almost falling off, what his master said came into his mind. **'You can fell an elephant with only your finger.'** As he pierced the tiger's eyes with his fingers, he fell on the ground. The tiger jumped here and there being terrified because of the pain as it couldn't see, and then it ran away. After that fight with the tiger, he stopped training and came down from the mountain. Since then, the man defeated all of his rivals only with his fingers and became one of the best."

Dennis was listening to him silently and asked him. "Could you teach me the finger technique?"

Dennis learned the finger technique from the man, and became the best in his school. One day Junior Dog tried the finger technique against Dennis but failed because of Dennis' glasses.

It is the technique that you sometimes can see in martial arts movies.
In some cases, when the technique is used in a real situation, the opponent might go blind. Thus you must use it in critical situations only.

Since the eyes are the largest nerve aggregate of the body, they say that a man can win a fight against an elephant or a lion if he pierces their eyes correctly. Everybody must have experienced tearful eyes and would not be able to see the front well when a small dust enters one's eyes.

If your opponent's eyes are pierced by your fingers and he cannot see the front, you will be able to win the fight very easily. Even though you face a big violent gangster, it's like you are fighting against a blind man as long as he cannot see what is right in front of his face.

Even though you are not strong, if you can gouge your opponent's eyes correctly with your finger, you can gain supremacy over him.

If your opponent can't see the front, you can always win the fight.

Long time ago, some people trained their fingers by a special method called 'Cheol Sa Jang', and used them as a cruel secret weapon to pull their enemy's eyeball out.

Cheol Sa Jang : One of the Hand Training Methods that makes hands strong just like iron.

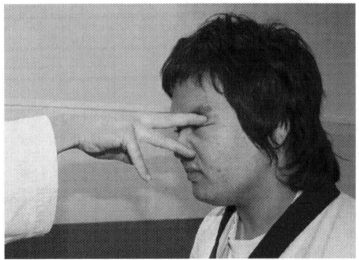

Sometimes it is abused as a cruel technique to pull the enemy's eyeball out.

Practice method

Unless you have an intention to pull your opponent's eyeball out, finger training such as Cheol Sa Jang may not be necessary.

Draw a face of person on a paper and attach it to the wall and repeat practice of piercing eyes with two fingers. Make sure the accuracy and speed when you practice it. After drilling two holes in a small box instead of paper, attach it on the wall and practice it.

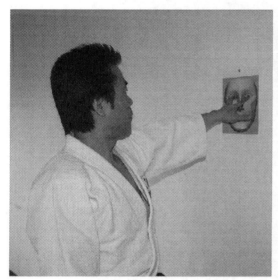
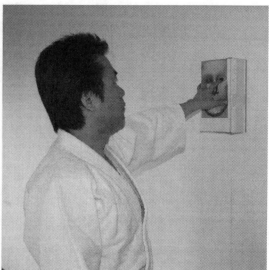

Practice with a paper   Practice with a box

The use of finger

Don't try to pierce the opponent's eyes with just two fingers. After unfolding all five fingers, practice piercing the opponent's eyes with the middle and index fingers.

It would be best if you can pierce your opponent's eyes correctly with the two fingers. However, in case you do not pierce your opponent's eyes correctly with the two fingers, you can pierce them with the other three fingers if you turn your hand.

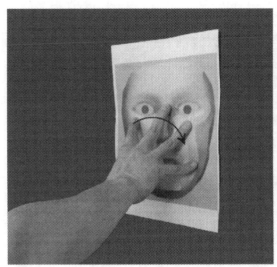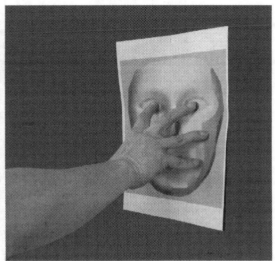

If you pierce incorrectly, turn your hand.   The other fingers will pierce.

The position of leg

It is good to maintain natural position. If you are a right-handed person, put your left foot forward. But if you are a left-handed person, put your right foot forward.

Left handed person
He puts his right foot forward

Right handed person
He puts his left foot forward

If you are putting your right foot forward, attack with the right hand. If you are putting your left foot forward, attack with the left hand.

When putting right foot forward   When putting left foot forward.

The closer the distance, the faster you can attack him.

Which hand is closer to the opponent?

Even Superman will throw in the towel by your front kick
- Striking Nangsim (groin)

I have stayed in Canada almost half a year. My parents and younger sister's family lived in Toronto, and it made me stay in Canada in early 1990. At that time, the streets looked empty due to the unusually cold weather and bad recession.

One day I was touring the downtown, carrying a camera on my shoulder. When I sat on a bench in a park to take a rest for a moment, one big man walked aimlessly up to me, and muttered something. I just stood up and asked him politely "I beg your pardon?" He made a grim face and raised voice. At the moment I felt myself being in danger, my leg flew up and struck the man reflectively in the groin which was between his two legs. As soon as the man toppled with a cry of pain, I left the place very quickly.

I just avoided the place because I did not want to be involved in a legal incident with the police. Moreover, Canada was a foreign land to me, and I was not able to communicate very well. Nowadays I can see news paper articles of firearm accident in Toronto area almost every day. Now, I know very well it was a dangerous situation which dealt with a matter of life and death. Whenever I think of that situation, I take a breath of relief.

We sometimes have the chance to face against a huge and dangerous person. If a weak woman meets with the molester of women like this, she cannot but be at a loss really. At this moment, just one Low Front Kick will deal with the situation. Dangerous situation will be over in a moment.

The Low Front Kick is the easiest one among all kicks. Even a baby can do it. A high kick needs a flexible body but there is no need to be flexible when using a low kick. It is not only an easy kick just like kicking a soccer ball but also a surprise attack as it is hard to make a mistake.

Low Kick is very easy just like kicking a ball.
Even a baby can do it.

Those who have two legs must widen their legs properly in order to stand with balance. The most stable stance is when you stand shoulder width apart. You cannot have a good balance when you stand with your feet together.

Standing shoulder width apart   Standing with feet together
You can have a good balance.   You can't get your balance

Everybody always stands his feet open in order to get a balance. Therefore, if you kick your leg straight towards your opponent, your leg will be sucked into the opponent's groin. As long as you try to miss your kick on purpose, there is no risk of missing it.

You can't miss it!

If you kick straight between the legs of your opponent, the last place the kick would reach between his legs is the Nangsim (groin), which is the weakest and most dangerous vital point of man. Even though he is Superman or Spiderman, he cannot help kneeling down when he gets hit in this area.

Practice method

Low Kick practice is very easy.

1. Imagine that your opponent is standing in front of you.
2. Kick him in the groin as quickly as possible.
3. Repeat this practice several times a day.

First, stand in front of your opponent in a natural position.

Second, keep the distance between you and your opponent as far as you can touch his body, and try your front kick as quickly as possible. At the distance where you can touch his body, you will hit your opponent's groin (Nangsim) correctly. As soon as you get the correct distance, try your front kick very quickly.

Always try to kick with your leg forward. The closer you keep the distance, the faster you can kick.

Which foot can kick the opponent faster, the left foot or the right?

The opponent who is hit on Nangsim must bend his body forward, and then hit his face with your knee. The game will be over.

Hit his face with your knee as soon as he bends his body forward.

Of course, you can use any other techniques to attack when he bends his body, such as kicking, punching and so on.

The Neck Strike that even Spiderman fears
- Tiger Mouth Hand Strike

It is called the Tiger-Mouth-Hand Strike because the shape of the hand looks like the mouth of roaring tiger.

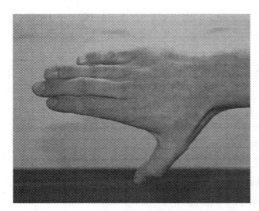

The shape of the hand looks like the mouth of a roaring tiger.

On the neck, there are a number of vital points. Thus, Eastern martial artists used to attack it in order to defeat their enemies. Tiger Mouth Hand Strike is one of the striking techniques for the neck attack. Since the windpipe is a dangerous part, this technique might even lead to death when it is hit hard. Hence you need to be careful when using this technique. Writing about it, I have a sudden flashback to my childhood.

These days, most Korean children must have the experience of training Taekwondo at gym. I am training Hapkido now, but the martial art that I trained for the first time when I was young was also Taekwondo. I lived with the uncles on the mother's side when I was young. It was an ardent wish of mine that I wanted to learn Taekwondo after seeing my youngest uncle, who was a black belt holder, exercise hard in YMCA gymnasium.

In the 1960s, since the gyms were relatively rare unlike now, it was difficult to learn martial arts. Only children who sincerely wanted to learn could register at the gyms. One day I asked my mother to register at the Taekwondo gym for me.

At the gym, I made friends with three elementary students of my age who entered before me, and enjoyed the exercise. We did fight-exercise in the gym every day at that time. We kicked and punched without any equipment for protection at our sparring. Now I think it was very ignorant and uncouth of us. Whenever returning home, my whole body was blue and black. I didn't care about it because I just liked doing the martial art. However, one problem occurred to me.

There was a boy who was quite big for our age. I used to be pushed around one-side by him whenever I was sparring with him. So I was mortified, and it hurt my pride. However, I got the opportunity to recover my pride. I learned one of the striking techniques, and it was a Tiger Mouth Hand Strike.

One day I used the technique on the boy's neck when I was being pushed around by him. The boy fell down on the floor and grabbed his neck, having trouble breathing. My revenge was fairly delightful, but I was given a terrible scolding from my teacher.

If you face a gangster by chance, can you beat him with a 540 degree turning kick? It is very splendid to see but almost impossible. The neck strike is one of the most powerful and simple self-defense techniques that you can use at any time when in danger. This technique is simple but as strong as the attack of tiger as you can beat an opponent with just one strike.

Practice method

Image training is quite good for the practice. Imagine that your opponent is standing in front of you. Stand in front of him and step forward and stretch out your arm and hit his neck with your hand making tiger-mouth shape.

Practice it using the front hand.

Which hand is closer to the opponent's neck?

You might be able to destroy your enemy's windpipe by holding it explosively with one thumb and four fingers as soon as you strike his neck. Such technique would be used on the purpose of killing the enemies in real fights long time ago.

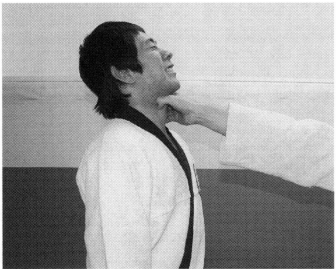

It can be used as a cruel technique to grab the opponent's windpipe and destroy it.

14

Why is Royce Gracie's hair, former UFC Champion, so short?
Tremendous powerful technique – Grabbing Hair

R oyce Gracie and most great fighters tend to cut their hair short because they know very well that it is very difficult for them to win the fight, especially when their hairs are grabbed by the opponents

I remember the scene that Royce Gracie grabbed Kimo Leopoldo's long hair and harassed him continuously at UFC 3 - The American Dream, September 9th 1994. Kimo was a strong and big fighter, but was getting tired and lost the fight by Royce's Arm Lock technique after all. At the moment, Kimo's long hair was a big trouble for him.

When most women start fighting, they try to grab the others' long hair. I think it is a natural phenomenon because long hair can be grabbed very easily. We can also find an interesting thing. When two women fight each other, one who grabs the other's hair first is likely to have an advantage at the fight.

The spine (vertebra) is located at the center of our body as it plays a significant role just like a pillar in our body. If someone holds around your neck (cervical vertebra) strongly with his arms, you can't move your body freely as you want. Sometimes a martial artist boasts of his power through throwing down a wild bull. He grabs the bull's horns with his both hands, and forces down the bull's neck. After being forced its neck down, the bull cannot use its power but just falls down on the ground.

If the cervical vertebra's nerve gets hurt by accident, the lower half of the body may become paralyzed. Muay Thai fighters seize their opponents' neck hard with both arms and shake it to destroy the balance, and then they deliver a knee attack. However, it's very difficult for an ordinary man to rush in and grab the other's neck.

Here is a method to achieve the control over opponent's neck easily. The easy method is to grab the other's hair.

Grabbing neck

Grabbing hair

If you are not a trained fighter, it's almost impossible to seize opponent's neck by your arms, but pulling the opponent's long hair with both hands is a piece of cake.

First, stretch out one hand, and snatch the opponent's hair quickly and pull.

Second, grab the opponent's hair with the other hand, and pull down his hair with both hands. If you keep the complete control over your opponent's neck, he cannot move as he wants.

Third, even if your opponent attempts to attack you, he can only hit in the air as long as you pull down his head.

Grab the opponent's hair with one hand.

Grab the opponent's hair with both hands.

He tries to hit you, but it is useless.

Strike the opponent's face with your knee while pulling down his head down. Your opponent would collapse only by your first or second knee attack.

You can attack with your knee.

Anybody cannot help giving up - Finger Lock

There are undesirable scenes that we can see very often when we drive out in Toronto these days. It is just what people raise their middle finger sky-high saying "Fuck you!" Yet it was rare to see them in the early 1990's when I visited there for the first time.

Compared to Seoul or New York, the traffic on the streets is not so bad, I think. I don't understand why people get so impatient and do this gesture. I am afraid to say but I have even seen not a few women doing this.

If someone raises his middle finger in front of your face and says "Fuck you!" how would you cope with that situation? Since you are insulted, you might think he must pay for that.

First, hold the opponent's middle finger very quickly, and pull it down.

 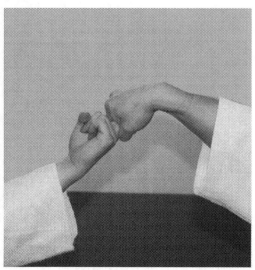

Grab the opponent's finger and twist.   Enlarged photo

Your opponent's body will naturally move to the direction where his finger is pulled.

You can move him as you want.

Second, as soon as you crush and pull his finger, shoot your head like a missile to his face at the same time.

Just one head butting is enough. The game will be over.

I am sure that no further attack is needed indeed.

Our body consists of large number of joints (116 joints) and there are over 3,000 joint lock techniques in Hapkido, one of the Korean martial arts. Finger Lock is one of the most powerful and easiest techniques among them, which nobody can resist.

20

Confuse opponent's concentration - Throwing something

Sometimes you face a very tough opponent to fight, who is perfect on his guard and very strong. How would you deal with it? First, you have to find out his unguarded points in order to defeat him.

People tend to duck instinctively if something flies fast toward them. However, if something is thrown slowly toward them, they might try to catch it instinctively in order not to let drop it on the floor.

You will avoid the ball if it flies fast toward you.   Instinctively you will try to catch the ball if it is thrown to you slowly.

This is an **Autonomic Reflex Action** taken before judging and acting.

In case you cannot find an unguarded point of your opponent, throw something lightly at him such as a bag, cap or any other things in your hand. The opponent would try to catch the thing instinctively, and an unguarded point can be detected at the moment. At this moment, carry out a preemptive attack by kicking in the groin (Nangsim-chagi) or something.

As you can see at the left photo, attack him throwing something you have. At the very moment he tries to catch it instinctively, you can find his unguarded point.

This is very useful fighting skill you can use first when you face an opponent.

Just one hit can finish the fight - Head Butting

One of the most interesting TV shows was International Professional Wrestling Title Match between the Korean team and the Japanese team, when I was a boy. There was a famous player, whom most Korean people liked very much. His special technique, which made the audience excited, was Head Butting. Almost every his opponent knelt down before him because of his Head Butting. It seemed like that there was no rival for him in the world.

The Korean team always lost scores in the beginnings of the title matches, but they finally got victories by his Head Butting at the end of the matches. Everybody would give a shout of joy to him and praise his greatest Head Butting, which seemed to have no rival in the world.

One of the strongest bones of a human body is skull. If someone is hit in his jaw by the other's head, it might cause a concussion of the brain, and he becomes unconscious and falls down. Also if he is hit in his face, the nasal bone can be fractured or some teeth can be broken. It is a very efficient technique for a short person against a tall person.

First, bend knees a little in near distance.

Second, stretch the knees shortly, and hit your opponent's jaw with your head. Sometimes there is a case in which they rush and hit the opponent's abdomen.

Jump and hit his jaw.   Rush in and hit his abdomen.

Just hitting an opponent's jaw is effective, but sometimes we can grab the opponent's collar with both hands and attack, or hold his waist and attack.

Grab his collar and hit.

Grab his waist and hit.

① If a molester of women hugs you in front

First, calm down without resisting. If you resist, he is going to hug you more strongly.

Second, lean your body on him. At the moment he feels that your body leans on him, he might relax his arm absent-mindedly, then you can move your body.

Third, bend and stretch up your knees, and hit his jaw with your head. Or, throw your head forward to hit him in the face.

Jump and hit.

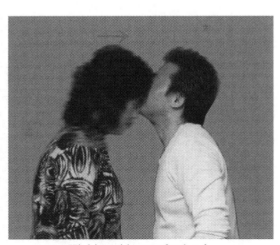

Hit him with your forehead.

Fourth, as soon as the molester looses his hug, escape quickly.

② *If a molester of women hugs you from behind,*

First, let him relax just like the above.

Second, bend and stretch up your knees to hit his jaw or face with your head. Or throw your head backward to hit him in the face with the back of the head.

Third, escape just like mentioned above.

Even a weak woman can knock out a strong man - Knee Strike

In fighting, there are four kinds of distances that one can strike his opponent.

1. Distance that the leg can reach
2. Distance that the fist can reach
3. Distance that the knee can reach
4. Distance that the elbow can reach

Leg touching distance   Fist touching distance   Knee touching distance   Elbow touching distance

Martial artists keep a distance in order to hit the opponents as they push and pull the opponents technically, and attack him using their legs, fist, knee or elbow properly according to the distance and situation.

In a close distance, Knee Strike is very powerful; so many martial artists often use their knees to attack their opponents in the distance.

Face attack   Belly attack   Side attack   Thigh attack

If a molester suddenly hugs a woman, who is weak and has never learned martial arts, what should she do? To make matters worse, she is in a situation in which she can't use Head Butting.

It is almost impossible for the woman to gain supremacy over the molester by any means even if she has learned martial arts for a long time. I am convinced that the technique below is the only way for her to escape this situation. The technique is Knee Strike for groin.

When a molester hugs you, at least one of your legs should place between his two legs. At this time, you can hit his groin (Nangsim) as you lift your knee.

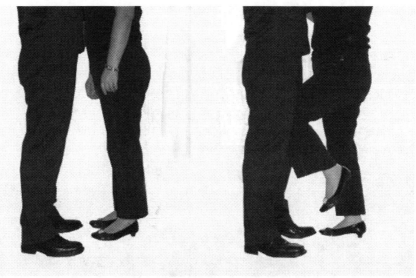

Just lift your knee; you can hit his groin exactly.

Since Knee Kick is one of the most powerful techniques, if one is hit in his groin strongly by Knee Kick, he could even be disabled. Since knee and the elbow would become a dangerous and powerful weapon, fierce fighting competitions often prohibit using them because of a deadly damage.

Bruce Lee would be surprised, and surrender – Striking Ear

When I was a high school student, I was a big fan of Bruce Lee. I saw all of his movies, and one of the movies still remains in my memories. The title was 'The way of the Dragon' and the scenery of the movie is Rome. In the movie, Bruce Lee and Chuck Norris fight in the Colosseum. Bruce is so fast that Chuck cannot strike Bruce correctly. Truly, Bruce is fast and well-balanced just like a cat.

However, what would happen if Chuck stroke Bruce's ear by his palm? I think Chuck might have won at the fight as soon as Bruce was hit in his ear because even Bruce would lose his balance.

Ear Strike is the technique that hits the opponent's ear by your palm. It is desired to use only in a critical situation because of the potential danger of exploding the eardrum.

If we unfold our palm, there is a cavernous part in the center of the palm.

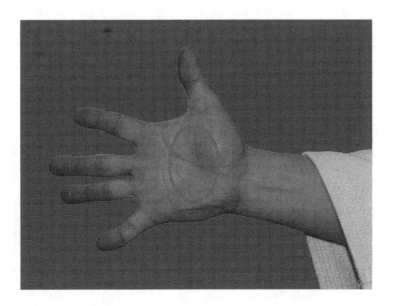

       This is the simple technique to put air pressure into the ear with the center part of your palm. It is important not to leak air at the striking time.

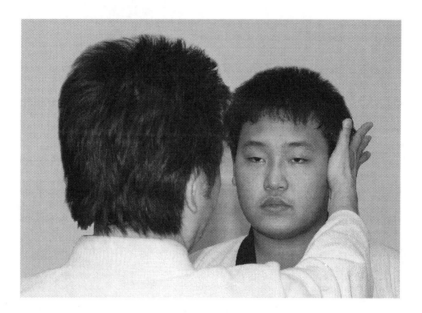

       When you hit an opponent's ear with your palm, the opponent loses his balance instantaneously and staggers because the eardrum and the cochlea, which take charge of the balance of the body, would get an impact by the air pressure.

       In case a molester hugs you in front, clap his ears with your hands. In case he holds your collar, clap his ear with your free hand.

Practice method

I think you don't have to practice this technique. Everybody can do it without Practice.

Unfold both hands, and clap them touching the middle sunken parts of the palms together. At this moment, pay attention and take care not to let the air escape from the hands.

Unfold your hands.

The middle sunken parts of the palms must touch together.

Saying it once more, never use this technique except in a critical situation because it might make him a deaf.

A key could be more dangerous than a knife - Key Attack

In 1960's, it seemed that there were many gangsters in Seoul. When I was a teenager, I had heard that my youngest uncle fought against three gangsters in a desolate back street. Even though he was a Taekwondo master, it was a little tough to fight alone against three gangsters who have knives. There was nothing with him except a house key in his pocket. He wrapped the key in his hand and extruded the key body between fingers, and blew punches. The gangsters got serious damages and my uncle was summoned to the police. Fortunately, my uncle was released because it was for a legitimate self-defense. When I heard that, I realized that a key could be more dangerous than a knife.

When I visited Hong Kong ten years ago, I saw Chinese monks practice throwing wood-chopsticks, and those chopsticks pierced through a wood board from the distance of about ten meters. Watching a martial arts movie, we can sometimes see a scene in which someone throws copper coin and it gets stuck in a wall. A long time ago, Eastern martial artists used to use things that were around them as weapons. In this chapter, I will introduce you how to use a car key or usual key as a weapon.

Even though you repeated practices for several years, it is not easy to use chopsticks or copper coin as a weapon just like in a martial arts movie. However, Key Strike is very easy for you to practice, and you can use the technique immediately.

Since this can also disable someone or lead him to death, it must be used just in case you are in a dangerous situation. Martial artists are able to use everything as a weapon, but even ordinary people can use a key as a horrible self-protection weapon through constant practice.

Women are physically inferior in strength compared to male attackers; moreover, they cannot carry a gun or knife all the time for self-defense. In a dangerous situation, it is impossible for women to confront men with empty hands. At that situation, they can use any key as a weapon.

Hold the handle of the key so that the protruding part of the key can stick out between your fingers, and make a fist. In case of using a car key, the key handle is made of plastic, so it feels comfortable to grab the key in the fist.

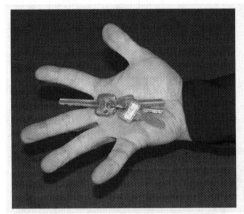
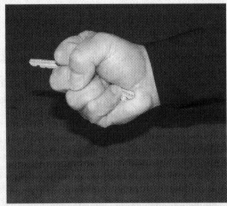

Unfold the hand and put the key on it.   Wrap the key with the hand.

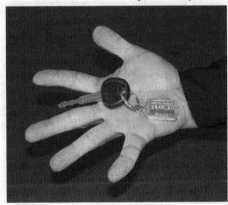
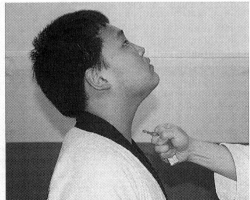

You can hit the exposed part of the attacker's (neck or face) with the Key-Fist.

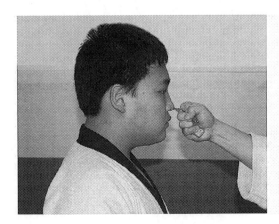

The exposed parts of the neck or the face are so thin and weak that they can be cut easily even by a light scratching. I will leave it up to your imagination how it is going to be if they are hit by Key-Fist.

If you hit the windpipe, carotid artery or eyes, the opponent might bleed to death. So use this technique just in case you or your family is in a truly dangerous situation.

A saw like key body can play a critical role to cut skin very widely.

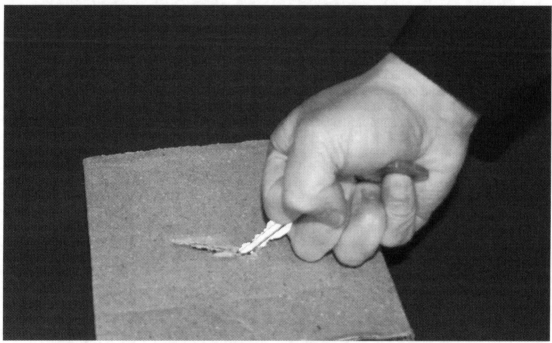

The Key Body can cut something like a saw.

If you extract the key sideways after hitting with the key, it could cut the surrounding vein. Thus, you must take precautions if you use it.

Icicle can kill someone – Ball-Point Pen Attack

There is a puzzle from a Korean story below.

'On a winter day, a case of murder took place in a public bath. A dead body was stabbed by something and shed blood on the bathroom floor. And the window was open. Detective Colombo investigated all over the public bath, but there was nothing at all - no marks, no footprint or no evidence of other people. Only the evidence was the dead body.

Detective Colombo wondered if it was a suicide because he couldn't find any clue for the death. However, Colombo was not sure. He stared at the open window, and smiled. "It's a suicide," he said confidently. Then, how did the man commit suicide?

Can you solve the puzzle above? The answer is an icicle hung from the roof outside the window. He was stabbed in his heart with the icicle, and the icicle melted away. Can an icicle kill someone? Don't be serious, it's just a puzzle.

Whenever I pass the airport inspection table to ride an airplane, I have one question in my mind "why are they doing this useless inspection?" It does not make any sense as long as they permit keys or ball-point pens because the keys can be changed into formidable killing weapons.

If terrorists practiced attacking techniques by using things around, which ordinary people can also use as weapons, for the purpose of terrorism for a long time, how fearful could this be?

Of course, everything can be changed into a terrible weapon. For example, when you break a plastic toothbrush, you can find the broken surface very uneven and sharp. If you stab someone's throat strongly with it, he might get a serious injury.

Most people carry a ball-point pen and it can be changed into a self-defense weapon for emergency. When you attack someone with a ball-point pen, the method of gripping a pen is same as the method of gripping a knife.

Usually, there are three knife grips.

1. Ice Picking Grip
2. Fighting Grip
3. Hitting Grip

| Ice Picking Grip | Fighting Grip | Hitting Grip |

In case of using a ball-point pen, attack with the Ice Picking Grip or the Fighting Grip because the target region would be the exposed neck or face.

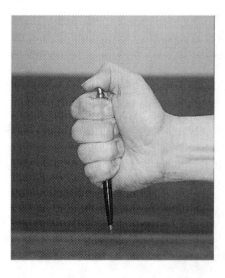

I don't recommend the Fighting Grip because ball-point pen is apt to be slipped in the hand when you hit the target with it.

Hold a ball-point pen with the Ice Picking Grip at the moment when you face an attacker. If he attacks from the front, hit the attacker's neck or face with the ball-point pen. Keep in mind that the attempt to hit the carotid artery on the neck or the eyes of your opponent could be a murder attempt.

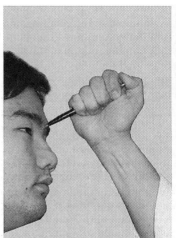 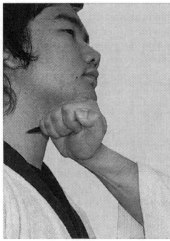 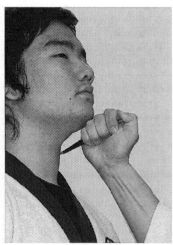

Eye attack   Carotid artery attack   Windpipe attack

The difference between Ball-Point Pen Attack and Key Attack is that Key Attack is able to cut skin but Ball-Point Pen Attack is only possible to pierce.

Fighting Grip as well as Ice Picking Grip can be used in the case of fighting against your opponent in a distance. Hold a ball-point pen in your right hand as you do for knife fighting. Keep your boxing stance, and disturb your opponent with your left hand aiming at his neck.

Disturb your opponent with your left hand.

It is easy to attack a fixed target. However, it is difficult to attack the neck of your opponent correctly, especially when he moves around a lot. So you need to practice it very hard. It is desired not to try this technique in a normal fight because it can endanger others' life. Just use it in a dangerous situation.

Nuclear bomb in your body - Elbow Strike

There was a student who exercised Elbow Strike very hard at the gym of master Dennis Kim. After daily training, he hits sand bag with his elbow for over 30 minutes everyday. Why did he do the Elbow Strike very hard like that?

Here is a secret story.

There was a bully in his classroom. The bully sat behind the student, and bothered him very often. One day, the bully started to bother him by pulling his hair from behind. The student couldn't stand it anymore, so he shouted at the bully "Don't do this!" and moved his arm backward in order to shake off the bully's hand.

At the moment, he felt something touch his elbow, and it became quiet. He looked back, and found the bully fallen down on the desk under unconsciousness. All the classmates were surprised, so they shook the bully and sprayed water on his face. After a few minutes, the bully recovered, and asked them with the moony face, "Something stroke my chin, and lightning flashed in my eyes and it became dark. What happened to me?"

"Sorry, I tried to shake off your hand, but hit your chin with my elbow by accident." said the student.

Since the student realized a power of Elbow Strike, he began to practice it very hard. After that day, the bully behaved carefully and stopped bothering others.

Elbow Strike is one of the powerful weapons we can use in a near distance. Even though being hit by the elbow lightly, soft skin like face can be cut easily.

Jaw attack　　　　　Temple attack

Rear neck attack   Side attack

① When a molester of women grabs your shoulder from behind,

Turn back rapidly, and hit his face strongly with your elbow. You will probably be surprised at the powerful effect.

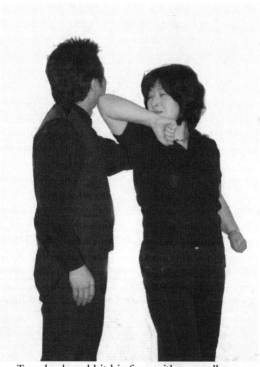

Turn back and hit his face with your elbow

② *When he grabs your shoulder with his hand from the front,*

If he grabs your right shoulder from the front, hit his face with your left elbow. Elbow Strike is very sharp like a razor as well as powerful, so the skin can be cut easily.

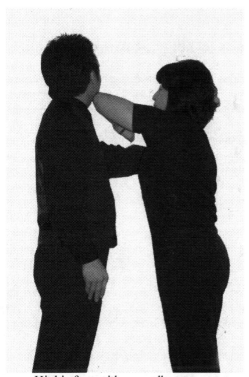

Hit his face with your elbow.

To be, or not to be: that is the question - Biting

I have a friend who is a talented Taekwondo master and had many experiences of attending international competitions as a national representative. One day, he told me an interesting story he had on a swimming beach during a summer vacation.

He went East Sea with his friends to enjoy summer vacation. There were many sexy girls on the beach, and muscular guys were walking around while showing off their robust muscle. When it became dark, they pitched a tent. After dinner, my friend strolled on the beach to enjoy a cool sea breeze.

Walking on the beach, he happened to see a man and a woman wrangling loudly. The man slapped her face all of a sudden, and the woman rushed to him cursing and damning. The man again slapped her face several times, and she cried out but nobody tried to pull them apart.

As my friend grabbed the man's arm to stop slapping, he stared at my friend angrily.

"Stop slapping her," said my friend. "It's none of your business. Just go your way," said the man. My friend didn't let go of his arm. Suddenly the man shook my friend's arm off, and wrapped my friend's neck with his arm. That happened in the twinkling of an eye, so my friend couldn't help it. He started to choke my friend's neck. My friend thought he must have been a wrestler or something, and realized he should try to escape.

Usually my friend could break a brick with his fist and break a baseball bat with his kick, but he was not good at grappling techniques. It was too late to escape from that situation, and my friend almost couldn't breathe. At the moment, there was no way to survive, except one.

My friend bit his arm mercilessly, and the man screamed sharply with a terrible pain. As soon as his arm got loose, my friend punched him continuously until he was knocked out. He shed blood in his arm, and fell down on the beach.

At the moment, a strange thing happened. "You, son of bitch, what the hell did you do to my husband?" the woman shouted, and rushed to my friend. Saying "What the hell is going on?" my friend was embarrassed, and ran away from the place.

Animals such as lions and tigers use their sharp teeth when they attack their preys. Their teeth are used to chew foods or to attack their preys as well.

Human teeth have become so degenerate that they can be used only to chew food. However, in a dangerous situation in which you have no other choice, the teeth can be a strong weapon even though it is a little dishonorable.

When the opponent is stuck on you to attack and you cannot use your arms and feet to escape, just bite him. Biting is one of the great techniques for attack that we have forgotten.

Horrible destructive power of the Body Twister
- Spin and Back-Fist Strike

This is a technique that I use often when I have a sparring with my student. It is not easy to escape because it is a technique for spinning and striking all of a sudden. Sometimes I attack two times in a row, following a guy who is stepping back.

When we hit someone, we usually hit with the knuckles. But this technique uses the Back-Fist (the back of the hand). If you suddenly spin in front of the opponent, he gets confused. At the same time, whirl your arm like a whip and strike his face with your Back-Fist strongly.

Spin suddenly clockwise, and strike his face with your fist.

It's a so sudden attack that he can't escape it. Sometimes you can strike with your arm instead of the fist, since it is as strong as Stick Striking.

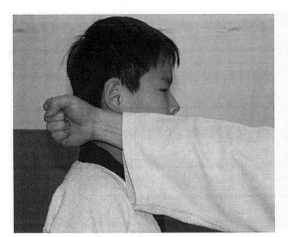 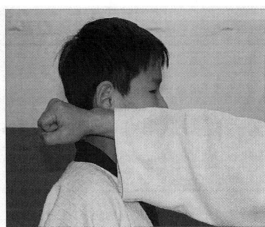

The target is opponent's temple, neck or jaw. You can hit with your Back-Fist, Hammer-Fist or forearm. If the distance between you and him is close, you can hit him with your elbow instead of your fist.

Even Arnold Schwarzenegger can't stand the pain
- String Ligament (Low Side Kick)

Westerners tend to have more progressed muscle than Orientals, and some people such as Arnold Schwarzenegger have muscle like an armor. A man with a good muscle looks so nice. In fact, our thick layer of fat and strong muscle can absorb some of the external impact forces, so they sometimes play a role in reducing damage.

But some parts of the body are not to be strengthened, even though we train very hard. Those are the eyes, nose, ribs, groin, chin, ligaments and so on. Among them, the cruciate ligament can be easily torn even during intensive training.

Knee Joint Ligaments

Anterior Cruciate Ligament (ACL)

Articular Cartilage

Lateral Collateral Ligament (LCL)

Femur

Medial Collateral Ligament (MCL)

Meniscus

Posterior Cruciate Ligament (PCL)

Fibula

Tibia

Left Knee From Behind

Cruciate ligament is a weak part that can be easily torn.

The Low Side Kick is a very simple technique that does not need much training, but the effect is great. The target of your kick is the opponent's knee. If he gets hit by your Side-Kick, he cannot walk due to the pain; moreover the leg can even be broken.

First, turn your body clockwise.

Standing position

Turn clockwise

Second, strike his knee with side-kick as fast as you can.

Lift your left leg.

Kick his knee very fast.

If your opponent is at a distance, you need to jump and kick. Your opponent has enough time to escape your kick because of the distance. So, this technique needs a large number of practices to kick very fast.

Step forward fast, and strike with Side Kick. You have to practice this motion over and over.

Strong muscle might absorb some of the external impact forces.

Killing punch without external damage
– Janggwon Chigi (Palm Strike)

They say 40 years is Bul Hok (the age free from vacillation), 50 years is Ji Cheon Myung (the age of realizing a mandate from heaven) and 60 years Li Soon (the age of promptly understanding what is heard) according to Confucianism.

I can't deny I also was hot-tempered until my thirties just like some other Koreans. When I was in my forties, I could control myself to some degree, as long as someone wouldn't threaten my life and family. Now in my fifties, whenever a trivial problem happens with others, I always try to apologize first.

I have never forgotten an incident I experienced when I was a university student. After training at the gym on a summer night, I waited for a bus to make my way home at the bus stop. It was so hot and humid that the Discomfort Index was very high. As I remember, there were about four or five people waiting for their buses.

Among them, one guy walked toward me. He staggered and smelled of liquor from his mouth, and the smell disgusted me. "Hey, lend me some money for bus," he said. I felt bad and wondered if he thought I was a chicken. "I don't know you at all, and have no money, either" I said bluntly. "How come you don't have money to lend me?" he said, and touched my body. "Oh, my God, he is crazy." I just hit his chin very fast and strongly with my palm, and saw him fall down on the ground. Everybody at the bus stop was surprised at the scene and just right at the moment my bus came. I hurried to get on the bus and left the place.

At home, I was worried about his condition and afraid the police would come to me. Fortunately nothing happened, but I felt awfully sorry for what I had done. He was just drunk and didn't hurt me. I should have been more patient. The memory of that day makes my heart bleed even today.

Eastern martial arts such as Hapkido, Taekwondo and Kung-fu have a technique called Janggwon Strike.

It is a Palm Strike technique.

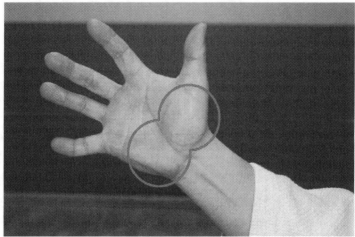

You have to use the part of your hand in the picture.
We call this part Janggwon.

Striking sandbag with Janggwon

In case you strike something with your fist, a fracture or injury might happen, but in case of striking with Janggwon, even though it gives a big damage inside, the damage cannot be seen from outside. If a martial artist, who has trained Janggwon Chigi for a long time, strikes another person's head with his palm, the man who was hit could die because it might cause a concussion of the brain without any external damage.

II. Self-Defense techniques in daily life

Various situations in Subway

We experience various things in various situations while living in global society. These various experiences sometimes involve in dangerous situations. Here, I would like to introduce some techniques to protect ourselves from these dangerous situations. Let's imagine whatever might happen to us.

① *You can have an unexpected incident on the subway platform.*

We sometimes see an article in a newspaper that someone fell on the rails, and got hurt seriously in the subway. There are so many people coming and going in the subway. Among them, there are some crazy people we call 'psycho'. Actually I have sometimes read articles where a psycho pushed someone onto the rails.

Carefulness would be the best way to escape such unexpected accident. When you stand at a subway platform, you'd better follow the direction below just in case.

First, stay far behind from the safety line. Even though a psycho would push you, you would have enough space to escape.

Second, if you stand at the front in the line, put your foot one step forward. Even though a psycho would push you, your forward foot would support you and prevent yourself from falling down.

You can't resist.   You can resist.

② When someone tries to touch your hip from behind

When there is a charming and glamorous woman in the subway, it is just a normal phenomenon for a man to give her a curious glance. But if someone loses his self-control and touches a woman's body secretly in a crowded subway train, it becomes a big problem because that is a sexual assault.

Women must cope with that situation wisely and bravely. If someone tries to touch your hip from behind, grab his finger and crush it.

First, grab his hand and scream loudly to let everyone know his sexual assault.

Second, just grab his finger and crush it mercilessly.

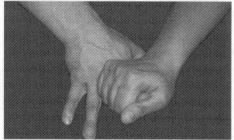

Grab his hand and then finger, and crush it strongly.

③ *When someone put his leg between your legs from behind*

There are even worse molesters than the one above. If someone puts his leg between your legs behind and try to touch your secret place with his lap, do like below without hesitation.

First, scream loudly to let everyone know his sexual assault.

Second, crush his foot strongly with the heel of your shoes.

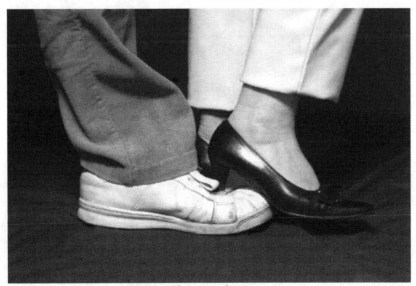

Close-up picture

He will limp for the time being.

Various situations you can experience while driving a Car

If someone tries to hurt you when you are in a car, lock the door and never go out. Call 911, if you have a cell phone. But we could be in the situations like below. I will introduce some methods to cope with them.

① Someone grabs your collar through the car window

First, put your left foot on the doorstep, and grab his arm with both hands.

Put your foot on the doorstep and support your body.   And grab his arm with your hands

Second, lean your body back, and pull him inside until he bumps against the door.

Lean your body back and pull his arm inside.

Third, push his arm into steering wheel and lock his wrist.

Lock his wrist by using steering wheel.

② *Someone opens the door and grabs your collar*

First, put your left foot on the doorstep and grab his arm with your both hands.

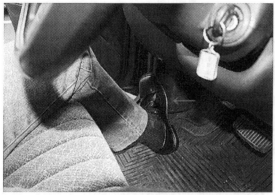

Put your foot on the doorstep and support your body.

Grab his arm with your hands

Second, lean your body back and pull him inside the car.
Third, Wrap his elbow with your left arm, and lock his elbow.

Pull him inside the car

Lock his elbow

③ *When you cannot avoid a rushing car*

When a driver, who is speeding up, finds a passerby walking on the street, even if he puts on the brake, the car cannot stop immediately but slides and might even crush the passerby. There are many serious car accidents because drivers sometimes don't see a passerby and just rush and crush people.

If you were unfortunately a passerby in that situation, what should you do? Would you just close your eyes and wait to die? I will introduce a way to save your life; however, it is not 100 percent reliable. Sometimes we can see a stunt man use this technique at a car accident scene in a movie.

If you see a car rushing toward you but can't avoid it,

Jump up and stoop yourself unconditionally. You will be rolled up on the car and fall down on the ground. You will probably get hurt but the probability of survival is high. If you are able to do a break-fall fortunately, the probability of survival would be higher.

If you are hit by a car directly,

First, you will probably get a serious unrecoverable damage on your body.
Second, your body will fly in the air and fall down on the ground.
Third, your head will probably be broken and you might even die.

Jumping aside is another very good way to avoid a car. If you are a professional, you can do it. But in case of emergency, it is a little more difficult for ordinary people (amateur) to jump aside than to jump up.

④ *Someone strangles your neck from behind*

Sometimes I see an article about murder case. For example, a taxi robber strangled a taxi driver to death from behind and robbed the money. In case we are standing, there are many techniques against a rear strangling attack. But if someone strangles your neck from behind while you are driving, you must be at a loss because you do not know what to do. Here I will show you the techniques of escaping from that situation.

There are three cases to strangle from behind.

First, Strangle with both hands
Second, Strangle with the arm
Third, Strangle with a string

Fortunately, headrest could be an obstacle for any attacker to strangle.

If someone strangles with both hands,

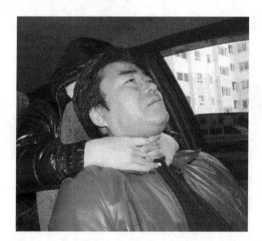

It is an easy case. You can grab his finger very easily. Grab his finger and break it strongly

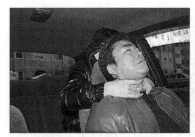
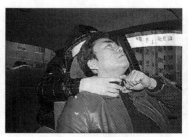
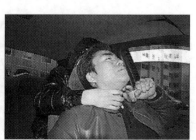

Someone strangles you　　　　Grab his finger　　　　lock his finger

If someone strangles with the arm,

No attacker can hold around your neck tightly with his arm because of the headrest. So, you can grab his finger. Grab his finger and break it mercilessly.

| Pull his arm with your hands | Grab his finger | Lock his finger |

If someone strangles with a string,

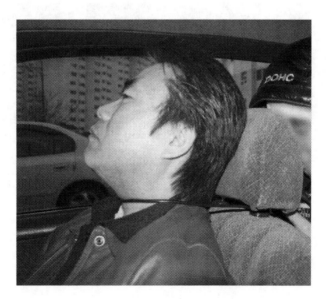

It is a difficult case. You have to grab the string with one of your hands and protect your neck before the attacker strangles you tightly.

With another hand, pull up the seat knob to put the driver's seat back to the maximum. This action is very important because this might make him lose his balance. If he does not lose his balance, it is almost impossible for you to escape that situation.

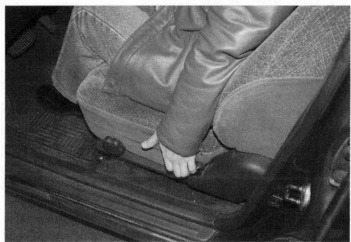

Pull up the seat knob and put the seat back to the maximum.

The attacker will lose his balance and cannot hold the string tightly as he wishes. Escape the situation with both hands.

Grab the string and pull up the seat knob.

Grab the string with both hands.

Escape the situation

Situations in office building

Sometimes we have a bad experience of falling down and being hurt even in an office building. Here I will introduce how to cope with it.

① When you miss your step on the stairs

Everybody once had an experience of missing his step on the stairs. If you hold the handrail, you can avoid a serious accident. But sometimes you could fall down on the stairs without holding the handrail.

If you miss your step on the stairs and fall down without holding the handrail,

First, stoop yourself when you start falling down.
Second, roll yourself aside as your body gets paralleled with the stairs.

Stoop your body at the moment when you are falling.

Roll yourself aside as your body gets paralleled with the stairs.

That is much safer than falling forward.

You can stop rolling in a while.

② *When your chair falls backward*

In Hapkido or Judo, students practice forward, backward, side and rolling break-falls whenever they train.

Forward break-fall   Backward break-fall   Side break-fall   Rolling break-fall

Break-fall is a very useful technique to protect your body when you fall down.

Of course, if you have time to practice, it couldn't be better. However, even though you only know the basic principle of break-fall, it will be very helpful for you when you fall down.

In Backward break-fall training, I urge you to raise your head and see the navel, and to strike the floor with both hands. Raising your head can prevent your head from being hurt, and striking the floor with both hands can disperse falling impact.

Almost everyone must have had an experience of falling backward with a chair at least once due to some reasons, such as while stretching the body with raised hands.

If your chair falls backward,

Raise your head and see your navel.

At the very moment you fall backward, raise your head and see your navel.

You can avoid a serious brain damage just by doing this action.

When you fight against a great kicker - Ankle Lock

As I mentioned before, the ligament is one of the parts which cannot be strengthened through training. You can make your muscle gorgeous and strong, but you can't do your ligament like that. The Achilles tendon is one of the weakest parts which can easily be torn while you are exercising.

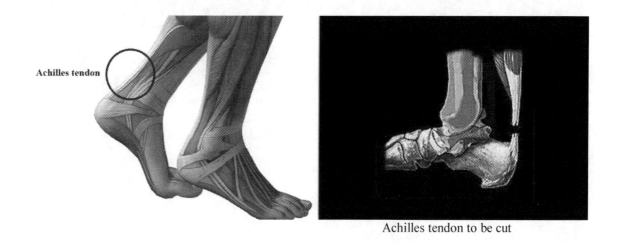

Achilles tendon

Achilles tendon to be cut

Sometimes you can get a chance to fight against a great kicker. Of course, the leg is more powerful than the arm, but kicking is slower than punching. While defending the opponent's kicking, you can have a chance to hold his leg. At that time, you can attack his Achilles tendon. In Hapkido, we call the technique 'Ankle Lock'.

If you hold the opponent's leg while he is kicking you,

First of all, throw him down.

| Hold his leg. | Hook the other leg. | Throw him down. |

As soon as he falls down, try the ankle lock.

First, hold his ankle with your arm, and put your forearm on his Achilles tendon.
Second, hold his ankle tightly with your arm and armpit.
Third, lean your body back and press his Achilles tendon with your forearm.

You can have three positions like bellows.

| Standing Ankle Lock | When he turns over | Sitting Ankle Lock |

Put your forearm on his Achilles tendon, and press it strongly with your forearm.

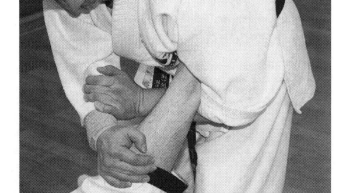

Close-up picture

When someone grabs your collar

U sually, grabbing the opponent's collar is the beginning of a fight. In case you are right handed, you usually grab the opponent's collar with your left hand and threaten him with your right hand.

There are many defense techniques against grabbing a collar. Here I will introduce you a simple one which you can do easily. There are two cases of grabbing, which are **Normal grabbing** and **Upper grabbing**.

① Normal grabbing

There are two techniques against normal grabbing.

(Technique 1)

First, grab his hand with your left hand.

Someone grabs your collar.

Grab his hand.

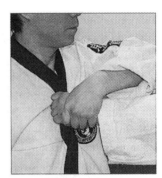
Close-up picture

Second, put your knife hand on his upper arm (triceps), twisting his left hand.
Third, step your right foot forward and push his arm down.

Put the knife hand on his arm

Step forward and push his arm down

Close-up picture

Forth, one more step forward, and push him down on the floor. Put your knee on his shoulder and press strongly. Lock his elbow and wrist.

Push him down on the floor, and lock his elbow and wrist.

(Technique 2)

First, grab his hand with your left hand, and his wrist with your right hand.

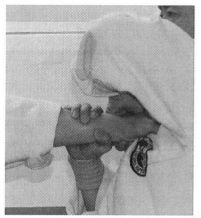

Close-up picture

Second, put his elbow in your armpit, turning your body counterclockwise.
Third, lock his elbow, pressing his elbow down.

Put his elbow in your armpit.　　Press his elbow down.　　Lock his elbow and wrist.

Close-up picture

② *Upper grabbing*

First, strike the crook of the opponent's elbow with your left knife hand. His body will lean toward you.

He grabs your collar upward.

Raise your knife hand.

Strike the crook of his elbow.

Second, grab his hair with your right hand, and his chin with your left hand.

Third, twist his head to the right side. The opponent should be thrown to the right side.

Grab his hair and chin.

Twist his head.

Throw him down.

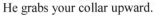

When someone mounts on you and tries to hit

In Hapkido sparring, when the opponent mounts on us, we consider it the worst position. It might be the same even in a real fight. However, unless the opponent who mounts on you is a professional grappler, you can turn the table very easily.

There are many techniques to escape this situation. Here, I will introduce a simple technique that everyone can do.

If an opponent mounts on your stomach and tries to hit you,

Someone mounts on you and tries to hit you.

First, grab his neck and one arm tightly so that he cannot hit you.

Second, bend your knees and put your foot on the ground firmly.

Third, raise your hips up, and push him towards his head.

Grab his arm and neck.

Bend your knees.

Raise your hip up.

Forth, he will lose his balance, and you can roll him sideways.

You have to roll him to the side where you grab his arm.

Roll him sideways.

The position would be reversed.

When someone tries to rape you

This is the worst situation for women. I hope that you will never face sexual assault but you'd better learn a technique to cope with such situation just in case.

Women are weak and tender, but the power of their legs is strong. Thus if they learn the defense technique as below, they would probably be able to control a man with their legs.

When a rapist throws you down, mounts between your legs and tries to rape you,

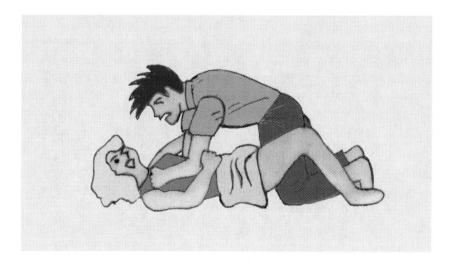

First, hold his wrists with your hands.
Second, raise your legs and put them on his shoulder.

Third, cross your feet together, wrap his neck and squeeze.
Forth, push his arms outside and lock his elbows.

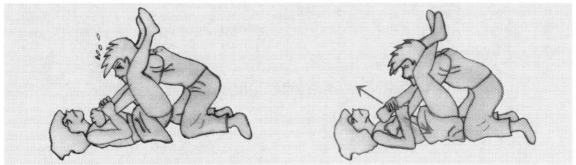

Hold his wrists, and put your legs on his shoulder.   Lock your feet and push his arms outside.

This is one of the Hapkido's techniques called Arm Lock. We usually use this technique in Guard Position. When the opponent falls down on the ground, try Lying Arm Lock.

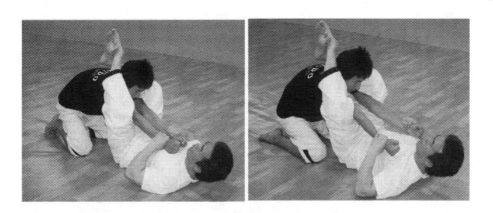

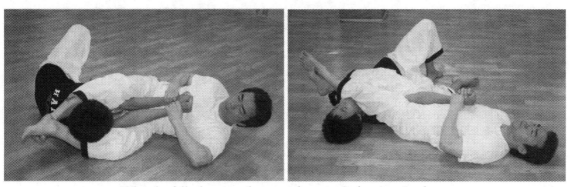

When he falls down on the ground, we try Lying Arm Lock.

There are some fighting rules

Everybody thinks that there is no rule in street fighting and it would be the best to win a fight by any means. I agree with that, but there are some rules in fighting you must know in order to win.

First, when your fight is about to start, you'd better stand at a higher place than your opponent. You can see his movement very well since the higher place makes your view widen. Also you can get a great advantage to attack him because it helps you make your stature higher.

Second, you should stand about two steps far away from him. Nobody can dodge the opponent's sudden blow even if he is one of the best fighters. So you need to stand about two steps far away from him.

If you stand close to him, it's very difficult to escape his sudden blow.

Third, look around attentively and try to find whatever you can use in the fight.

If there are sands on the ground, you can spray them into your opponent's eyes when you are out on a limb.

Forth, you'd better avoid fighting, especially against more than two people. We can see a movie that a hero beats many gangsters gorgeously. However, in fact, it is very difficult to fight against many people and win.

If you can't avoid fighting against many people, make sure that you let them stand before you and try to knock down the weakest one first, and another, one by one.

Physiologically, human physical strength has a limit. Sooner or later, you will get so exhausted that you can't fight any more.

Never let them stand behind you.

Fifth, never fight against a man with a weapon such as a knife or a gun. Even though you are the better fighter, it could be a suicidal act to fight against a man with a weapon. In this situation, running away would be the best self-defense technique. But if you can't escape for some reason, you must defeat him. I will introduce some techniques to cope with this situation at the next lesson, **'Knife attack & defense'**.

Sixth, if a street fight starts, you must have a mental attitude that you will win by all means. In a fight, such state of mind would be more important than any other fighting techniques. Physical strength and fighting techniques are the next to be considered.

When someone grabs your wrists from behind

I f someone attacks you from the front, you can respond to it easily, but rear attack is different. Moreover, if both of your hands are grabbed, the situation can be more serious. Not only your punch but also your kick becomes useless.

If someone grabs your wrists from behind,

First, raise your right hand up a little. This is a fake motion in order to move your left hand.

Second, raise your left hand up, and drop your right hand down, stepping your right foot backward.

Someone grabs your wrist
from behind.

Raise up your right hand.

Drop down the right hand and
raise up the left hand.

Third, grab his wrists with your hands and X twist his arms

Forth, straighten your body.

Fifth, Step forward with your right foot. Push on his right hand and pull on his left. Throw him down.

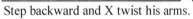

Step backward and X twist his arms.   Close-up picture   Throw him down.

When someone hugs your body with his arms

There are two types of Bear Hug Attack. One is a Frontal Bear Hug and the other is a Behind Bear Hug. Below are the techniques to escape those situations.

① When Frontal Bear Hug

There are two techniques

(Technique 1 -Twist head)

First, hold the opponent's hair with your left hand.

Second, hold the opponent's chin with your right hand, and twist his head.

Third, throw him down.

Hold his hair and chin.

Twist his head.

Twist it continuously.

Throw him down.

(Technique 2 -Chin push)

First, hook around his waist with your right hand.

Second, open your left hand and push it on his chin.

Third, push him back explosively.

Hook his waist.

Grab his chin.

Push his chin.

Throw him back.

② *When Behind Bear Hug*

There are three techniques.

(Technique 1 -Wrist lock)

First, grab his right fist with your both hands. Sit down a little, and twist his fist clockwise.

Someone hugs you from behind.   Grab his fist with your hands.   Sit down and twist his fist.

Close-up picture

Second, lock his wrist joint continuously, and turn around. Kick his face with your foot.

Lock his wrist joint and turn around.

Lock his wrist continuously.

Kick his face.

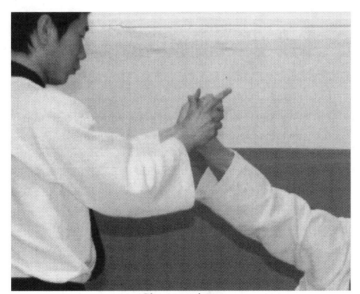

Close-up picture

(Technique 2 -Leg Lock)

First, widen your right leg, and let his right leg put between your legs.
Second, bend your body forward, and hold his right leg.

Widen your right leg.   Bend your body and hold his right leg.

Third, straighten your body fast, pulling his leg up.
Forth, sit down on his knee, and lock his knee.

Straighten your body, pulling his leg up.   Sit down on his knee, and lock his knee.

(Technique 3 -Middle Finger Fist Strike)

Below is the picture of Middle Finger Fist.

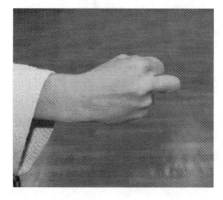

This Middle Finger Strike gives not a big damage but a serious pain. We usually use this Middle Finger Fist to hit the philtrum or the solar plexus.

Hit the back of his hand strongly with the Middle Finger Fist. He will feel a terrible pain and release his hug.

Raise your fist.

Hit the back of his hand.

Close-up picture

Can you imagine the pain? Try Middle Finger Fist Strike on the back of your hand. You can feel the terrible pain.

When someone chokes your neck with his arm

There are two types of neck holding attack. One is **Guillotine choke** and the other is **Headlock**.

Below are the techniques to escape those situations.

① Guillotine Choke

Guillotine Choke is to choke someone's neck with the forearm blade.

There are two techniques to escape the Guillotine Choke.

(Technique 1 – Throw down)

First, put one of your hands between opponent's legs, and hold his shoulder with the other hand.

Second, lift up and throw him down.

If you throw him onto your knee, it can be very devastating. His backbone and ribs can be broken.

(Technique 2 – Wrist Lock)

   First, grab his fist with your right hand, and his elbow with your left hand.

   Second, raise your head pushing his fist. When you push his fist, his wrist will be twisted.

Grab his fist and elbow.   Raise your head pushing his fist.   Close-up picture

   Third, grab his hand with your both hands.

Forth, put your right foot 45 degrees forward, and put your left foot backward. Lock his wrist continuously.

Grab his hand with both hands　　　　Step forward　　　　Turn your body counterclockwise

Fifth, put your right foot backward, pressing his elbow down with your right Knife Hand.

Put your left leg on his elbow, and twist his arm.

Put your right foot backward pressing his elbow.　Put your left leg on his elbow, and twist his arm.

② Headlock

As soon as the opponent holds your neck, he will probably try to throw you down on the ground. So, you should defend yourself trying not to fall down.

First, grab his left upper knee with your right hand in order not to fall down.

Second, hold his left shoulder with your left hand, and put your left knee on the crook of his right knee.

Third, pull your left hand backward and push your left knee forward at the same time. Throw him down.

Grab his knee and shoulder. Put your knee on the crook of his knee, and pull his shoulder backward.

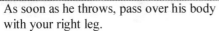
As soon as he throws, pass over his body with your right leg.

Wrap his body tight with your right leg.

Forth, pass your right foot over his body, and wrap his body tightly. Make your base firmly.

Fifth, put your left arm blade on his neck, and make Figure Four grabbing your left wrist with your right hand.

Sixth, press his neck strongly, stretching your arms.

Seventh, hold his right arm tightly with your left arm.

Put your arm on his neck, and make Figure Four.

Straighten your right arm, and press his neck strongly. He will release your neck.

Eighth, hold his right arm tightly with your both arms.

Ninth, pass your left leg over his head, lie back.

Tenth, press his head and body with your feet. Lock his elbow, pulling his right arm down and lifting your hips up.

Hold his arm tightly with your both arms.   Different angle view

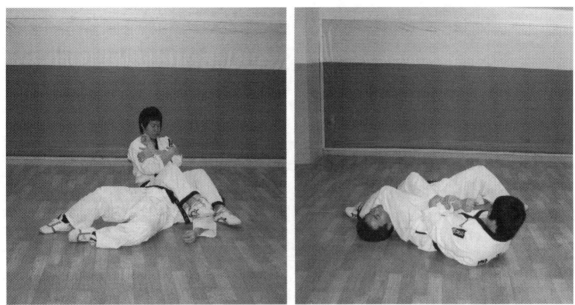

Lie backward, and lock his elbow strongly.

We call the above technique Cross Arm Lock. You have to drive your knees tight together when you try this technique. Sometimes he pushes your left leg over his head, and tries to escape. So you had better cross your legs firmly.

Break-fall (Safe way of falling down)

I take a trip abroad very often with my wife. This summer, we went to Hinam Island, which is located at the south-west of China. Summer climate of the area was more humid and hotter than Seoul as it has a tropical climate just like Guam. I had a very dangerous accident there.

It was a big city but there was only one traffic signal in the city. It looked not only dangerous to cross the street but also very strange to me. Everybody who travels here first might feel the same as I do. In order to cross the street, we had to watch carefully the both sides of the street and ran fast. There were fences on the middle of the street to prevent people from crossing the streets, where there were no crosswalks.

I was touring around the city and bought some tropical fruits. I checked both sides of the street to cross and saw some cars coming from a distance. I ran fast through a crosswalk. Suddenly I felt something hit my shin strongly, and fell down forward in the middle of the street. My hands hit the street, and my fruits poured out of the plastic bag. Fortunately the cars stopped.

What had happened? I rose up and looked back. Oh my god!! There was an iron pipe, about 5 inches in its diameter, in the middle of a crosswalk. It was painted with white stripe, and the crosswalk was painted with white stripe too. I couldn't see it while I was in a hurry. Perhaps they established it not to turn a car through a crosswalk. Everything was beyond my common sense. Anyway I felt serious pain on my shin, but fortunately it was not broken.

What if I didn't hit the street with my hands first? What would have happened to me? My face might be crushed and got a serious damage. The action that I did when I fell down forward is a kind of Forward break-fall. When we fall down, our body does a kind of break-fall action instinctively.

If you learn and understand about the principle of break-fall, it will help you protect yourself from any danger, especially when you fall down accidentally.

① *Forward break-fall*

This technique protects your face from a serious damage.

<Practice>

First, kneel down on the floor.

Second, fall on the floor.

Third, turn your face to the side, and hit the floor with your hands. When your hands hit the floor, the impact of falling will be dispersed.

Forth, jump and put your foot backward, and straighten your body out.

② *Backward break-fall*

This technique protects your head from a serious damage when you fall backward.

<Practice>

First, hunker down on the floor.

Second, fall backward seeing your navel, and hit the floor with your hands.

After you train the brake-falls for a long time, you will be able to jump and fall backward on the ground safely. There are many break-fall techniques, but the two techniques I have introduced above are the basic ones which everyone can do easily.

III. Knife attack & defense

Basic principles of knife fighting

A knife is a very useful kitchen tool in our life. But on the other hand, it can be changed into a very powerful weapon in a dangerous situation. One of the weapons we can get easily in our surroundings is a knife.

The knife used in the kitchen is not manufactured for killing and injuring, but when it is used in a violent fight, it could be changed into a formidable weapon that can kill other people. When a burglar breaks into your house, if you have a gun, it can surely help you protect your house from the burglar. However, even if you don't have a gun, a knife in your kitchen might help save you from the danger. In this situation, you should also keep in mind that if you don't know how to use it, it will even make yourself dangerous on the contrary.

Knife fighting is so different from hand-to-hand fighting because it can be a matter of life and death. In a knife fighting, to live or die depends on whether you know the principles following or not. Keep these principles in mind.

First, in case you face a man who has a knife, the best defense technique is to run away from that place unconditionally. It may become a reckless challenge if you try to gain supremacy over someone who has a knife, no matter what a great fighter you are. Moreover, if he is an excellent user of knife, you must prepare for death.

Second, unless you are an expert of knife, never lead with a knife when you are within striking range. If you extend your knife hand, he can grab your arm or kick your hand holding a knife.

Never lead with your knife.

He can grab your knife.

Or he can kick your knife.

Third, never get entangled and fall down together with your opponent who is holding a knife. As soon as you fall and lose a balance, he might try to stab your body with a knife without hesitation.

Forth, even great fighters can get hurt in a fight. Keep in mind that you might get hurt and bleed in a knife fighting. Everybody becomes nervous when he sees himself bleeding, and being nervous can be a danger for you. Try to calm down all the time. You must learn how to control your fear.

Fifth, if possible, don't fight with your bare hand against someone with a knife. If you don't have anything in your hand to cope with a knife, look around the surroundings and try to find something to resist against the knife such as stick, chair, candlestick, etc. Take it and fight with it.

Sixth, in case you have a knife, never extend your hand holding a knife, except for stabbing your opponent. Whenever you extend your hand, your opponent has an opportunity to counterattack you.

Seventh, you have to keep moving during the knife fighting. It is difficult to hit a moving target. Try to move continuously while keeping your proper distance. Avoid exaggerated movements, and keep your balance while moving.

Now I will explain the basic knife attack techniques and defense techniques to protect your life.

Knife attack technique

There are two types of knife attacks.

First; attack to stab other people.
Second; attack to scare other people.

If you are not a special-forces agent, you don't have to learn the **first technique**. Most robbers just threaten people in order to take other's properties. Your goal is to prevent your property from robbers, not to stab the robber with a knife.

If you face someone who uses the first technique, the purpose of his attack would not be money but to kill you. I am sure you won't have such an experience as long as you are an ordinary person. However, you might face with the situation that you have to stab someone unwillingly in order to protect your life.

① *Attack to stab other people*

If he is a knife specialist who has the purpose to kill someone, he will never stick a knife out in front of someone, except for having a best chance to stab. It's because this action can give an opportunity for his opponent to counterattack the hand that holds a knife. The knife specialist will hold his knife hand very closely to his side until he can find a right opportunity to stab.

If you inevitably attack to stab someone with a knife,

First, bend your knees, lean your waist forward a little and check him with your empty hand, maintaining the boxing stance. Keep holing the knife in your hand close to your side until you get a chance to attack.

Keep holding the knife in your hand close to your side.

Second, while keeping on breaking up his concentration with your empty hand, stab him with a knife as quickly as you get a chance (try to grab his arms or legs).

As soon as you grab his arm, stab him quickly.

As soon as you grab his leg, stab him quickly

Attacking target is the neck or the trunk area below the lung. They might aim for the heart, but knife can be sometimes blocked by the ribs and is apt to rebound from the breastbone. Thus, stabbing trunk area many times would be more effective.

② Attack to scare other people

If someone puts his knife forward threatening other people, he must be either an ignoramus or a knife specialist. Knife specialist uses slashing technique before stabbing, so he often puts the knife forward.

If a novice of knife fighting puts his knife forward to use a slashing technique, he will get a risk. Whenever his hand is extended for slashing, his opponent is going to try to kick his knife or grab his hand holding a knife.

Knife defense technique

When you face someone who holds a knife, the best defense technique would be to avoid that place as I have mentioned several times. But if you can't avoid the place, remember the below.

First, find any object that can be used to fight against the knife, such as stick, chair, candlestick, etc. It is dangerous to stand with bare hands. You must find and hold something to resist around where you are.

Second, do not get tangled and fall down together with the opponent who is holding a knife. This is the most dangerous situation when you fight against someone with a knife. At the moment he and you are very close or he holds you, he will probably try to stab you with his knife without hesitation.

Third, keep in mind that the primary target for knife attack would be the groin, eyes or throat.

Nowadays, many people, who enjoy watching TV or movies, have vain imagination about knife fighting. In television, we can see an unarmed hero disarm and beat up bad guys very quickly and easily. Usually bad guys cannot even have a chance to resist. However, real fight is different. As knife fighting is a matter of life or death, it can be much more different. There is a significant difference between the reality and imagination. So absurd knife defense techniques might even help you expose yourself to danger.

Now I will explain some of knife defense techniques that are taught at martial arts gyms. Remember that most of the knife defense techniques being taught at the gyms are usually for the cases in which you fight against an amateur of knife fighting. The defense technique against a knife specialist is a different story.

You have to practice it over and over until you can do it with closing your eyes.

① *When someone rushes on you to stab your body*

If someone rushes on you to stab your body and there is no way to avoid,

First, turn your body clockwise and avoid the knife.

Second, grab his wrist with your left hand, just like hitting downward.

Third, turn your body clockwise, putting your right foot backward.

Forth, pull his knife wrist downward strongly.

He rushes upon you to stab.   Turn your body, and grab his wrist.   Pull his wrist down strongly.

Close-up picture

Turning your body is the most important action to defend knife attack.

When he tries to stab you, you should turn your body at the same time. Then you wouldn't get any fatal wound. The knife cannot pierce your body because your body is turning. Even though the knife touches you, you will get only minor scratch.

Fifth, grab his hand with your right hand and lift his knife hand up with your both hands.

Sixth, turn your body counterclockwise putting your left foot forward.

Seventh, twist his knife wrist with your both hands.

Grab his knife hand with your hands, and twist it.

Close-up picture

② ***When someone tries to stab your neck from overhead,***

There are three defense techniques for this.

(Technique 1)

First, step closer to the opponent's body, and block his knife hand with your left arm.

Second, turn counterclockwise, wrapping around his knife arm with your right arm.

Third, put your back onto his body, and pull his knife arm forward.

Rush into him, and block his knife arm.

Step in and turn your body, wrapping his arm and pulling his knife arm forward.

Forth, lift his body up.

Fifth, throw him down.

Sixth, take his knife from his hand.

Put your back onto his body.

Lift him up, pulling his knife arm.

Pull his knife arm continuously, and throw him down.

(Technique 2)

First, step closer to him and block his knife arm with your left arm.

Second, wrap his knife arm around with your right arm from top to bottom.

Step forward and block his knife arm. Wrap his knife arm around.

Close-up picture

Third, put your right foot forward pushing his knife arm down.

Forth, throw him down.

Step forward and push him down.   Throw him down.

Close-up picture

③ *When someone threatens with a knife behind your back,*

    First, turn your body clockwise quickly, and strike his knife arm slightly with your right arm.

    Second, grab his knife wrist with your left hand, just like hitting downward.

Someone threatens you.

Turn your body clockwise.

Strike his knife arm slightly, turning your body.

Grab his knife wrist with your left hand.

This time, even if your opponent tries to stab you, you will never get a fatal wound but might have a little scratch because your body is turning.

Third, turn your body clockwise 180 degrees quickly putting your right foot backward.

Forth, grab his knife hand with your right hand pulling his knife wrist upward.

Fifth, twist his knife wrist with your hands putting your left foot forward.

Turn your body, pulling his knife arm.

Pull his knife arm upward.

Twist his knife wrist with your both hands.

Throw him down.

Close-up picture

Close-up pictures

④ *When someone threatens you, shaking a knife to slash,*

If you don't know any defense techniques at all and there is nothing around you to cope with the knife, followings are some ways you can do. But frankly speaking, I don't want to recommend these techniques, because they are not perfect.

(Technique 1)

First, take off your jacket, and shake it before him to confuse his concentration.

Second, kick or grab his knife arm as soon as you get a chance. Fortunately your jacket could hit his knife, and make him drop it.

(Technique 2)

Lie on your back against the ground, and resist the knife with your feet. Fortunately your feet could hit his knife, and make him drop it.

Mental Self-Defense

IV. Danjeon Breathing

The meaning of Danjeon Breathing

Spiritual stress that we cannot see threatens us in modern society as well as a violent bodily crime. As a society develops, Violence becomes atrocious while our life becomes abundant, and the stress that we receive in a complicated society disturbs our spiritual life and is destroying our health.

In modern society, Mental Self-Defense to protect us from an external stress as well as Body Self-Defense against an external violence is very important. There are Self-Defense techniques to protect our own from the spiritual stresses. We call them Mental Self-Defense techniques, and one of them is **'Danjeon breathing'**.

When babies are born, the first thing they do is crying to breathe. Human being starts their life on the earth with breathing. While you are breathing, you take not only Oxygen but also **Ki** from the air.

What is **Ki**? To say simply, it is **'Inner Power'**. Oriental doctors think that sustaining our life is **Ki** and if **Ki** is exhausted entirely from our body, we shall die. Bible says in Genesis 2 "Then the Lord God formed man of dust from the ground, and breathed into his nostrils **the breath of life**; and man became a living being." Whenever I read this Biblical quotation, I feel interest in that. I think **'the breath of life'** in Bible might be **Ki**.

To my regret, we cannot see what it looks like, and just can feel it. Many people have tried to prove the existence of Ki, but nobody succeeded. In 1977, there was a trial to measure the amount of Ki that was radiated by a Ki trainer with electromagnetic waves instrument in China. Through these trials, we can imagine that Ki is a kind of Wave. All beings in the universe have their own number of vibrations, and so have human being. Ki probably help our number of vibrations to be stable.

Danjeon Breathing is the way of taking **Ki** through breathing. Very simply stated, Danjeon Breathing means '**abdominal breathing**'. When you were a baby, you breathed through abdominal movement. But as you become a grown-up, you breathe by chest movement. We forget abdominal breathing, and in the result, our body is getting shorter of **Ki**. Through Danjeon Breathing, we can get not only a body health but also mental health.

Danjeon Breathing is the most basic and important practice in Eastern medical art and martial arts. Because the way of Danjeon Breathing is very deep and wide, I will summarize it very easy in order for the ordinary people to practice effectively.

Danjeon Breathing is a strong and mysterious Mental Self-Defense technique. When someone is taken ill, western doctors examine the disease closely and find out what kind of bacteria cause the disease and write a prescription to kill the pathogenic bacteria. Whereas Easterners think a disease of the body comes from the imbalance of **Ki**, so they give a prescription and acupuncture to accomplish the balance of **Ki** for the patient.

In former days, occurrence of illness depended on physical factors, such as dirty living environment, malnutrition, etc. Whereas in modern society, people live in clean and abundant living environment, and occurrence of illness depends on spiritual factors, such as stresses from the complicated civil life.

Danjeon Breathing is an Eastern traditional breathing technique. Easterners are able to keep their spiritual health as well as bodily health by receiving their insufficient **Ki** from the outside.

Everything on the earth, living things or lifeless things, consists of molecules. If we observe the human body through an electron microscope, it seems like a **small universe** being consisted of a lot of atomic nucleuses and electrons. The Universe where we live is managed by God's mind. Our spirit is the god of this small universe, and the small universe, our body, is managed by our mind (spirit). If our mind becomes unstable because of mental disorders, our body and spiritual health will be getting worse. Therefore, to defend our mind from spiritual stresses is very important.

Ki is the **inner power** that makes our body move. So **Ki** plays a major role for us to live healthy. We can get **Ki** from the Universe, and our mind can use it as the mind wants. In our body, there are 12 meridian pathways (Kyung Rak) that **Ki** flows through. Even though we cannot see them though our eyes, it seems like the veins that run in our body.

There are 365 depots on Kyung Rak, and we call these Acupuncture Spots (Kyung Hyul). Oriental doctors acupuncture on these places. One spot of them is Danjeon and it is situated 3-5 cm below the navel.

Ki flows continuously through Kyung Rak. Something wrong in the flowing leads to imbalance of health. You can regain the health and well being by restoring the Ki. Acupuncturists, massage therapists and Chinese herbalists can help you to repair dysfunctional areas by utilizing various healing methods.

The picture of next page shows Kyung Rak and Kyung Hyul.

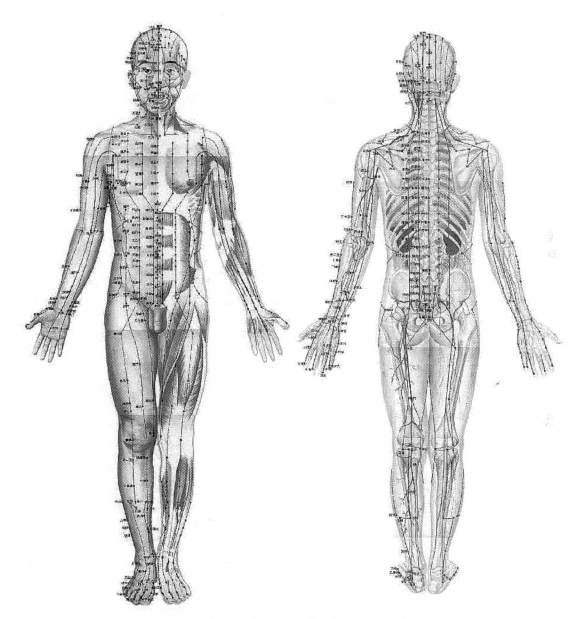

Picture of Kyung Rak and Kyung Hyul

A baby who is born in the world takes Abdominal Breathing (Abdominal Respiration) to push out and pull in the belly. This is a natural image of Danjeon Breathing.

People take Lung Breating (Thoracic Respiration) piecemeal while they are growing, and the breath is getting short and shallow. In the air, there exists not only **Ki** but also oxygen which is very important for life extension.

Now let's try Danjeon Breathing.

First, push the belly out.

Second, breathe in. (oxygen and Ki are coming together.)

Third, pull the belly in.

Forth, breathe carbon dioxide out. At the same time, send **Ki** into Danjeon, and accumulate **Ki** at Danjeon. That is Danjeon Breathing.

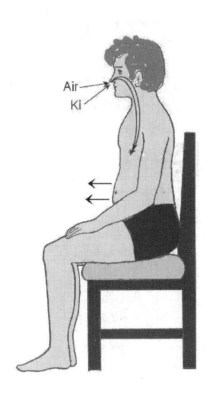 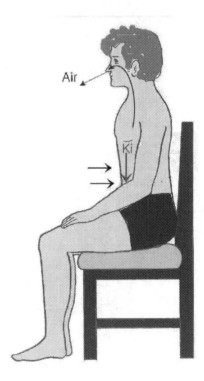

Method of Danjeon Breathing

I t is very important to relax your stiff body before Danjeon Breathing. Body relaxing helps **Ki** to flow very well.

Now I introduce **Ki exercise** to relax your body.

< Ki exercise >

① Shake your hands off

Relax your body and shake hands off, from up to down. It makes your body soft and relaxed.

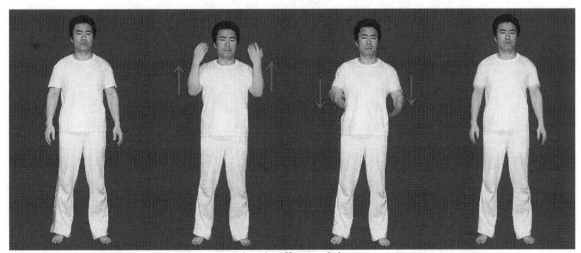

Shake your hands off several times

② *Neck exercise*

Lean your head to rear and the front, right side and left side. And rotate. It is good for your respiratory organ and **Ki** circulation promotion

Lean and rotate your head.

③ *The side exercise*

Raise your right hand and stretch your right side, Switch directions. It is good for your lumbago.

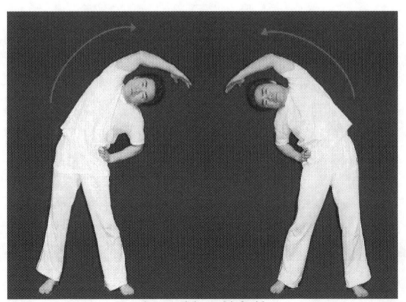

Stretch your right and left side.

④ *Trunk spinning*

Raise your arms, and rotate your trunk right and left side. It makes your waist soft.

Raise your hands and rotate your trunk right and left side.

⑤ *Rub and bend knee*

Think that Ki in your hands makes your knees soften when you rub your knees.

First, rub your knees to the arrow direction.

Second, sit on your legs and straighten your legs

.

It prevents arthritis.

Rub your knees to the arrow direction.   Bend and stretch your knees.

⑥ *Leg stretching forward*

Put both legs out front, and lean the body forward. Lean your body slowly, breathing out. Lean forward until you feel the tension of the muscles of your rear legs.

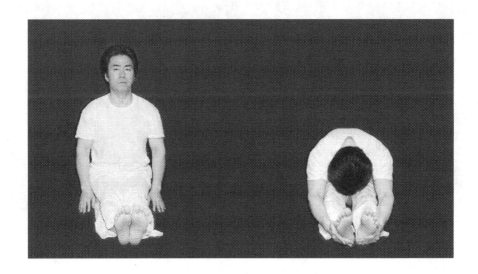

⑦ *Open legs stretching*

Widen your legs as far as you can. Stretch, and reach forward with both hands.

⑧ *Legs tapping*

It helps **Ki** circulation promotion

First, tap your right thigh from up to down, and on the contrary.
Second, tap your left thigh from up to down, and on the contrary.

Tap your right thigh

Tap your left thigh

⑨ Knees hugging and rolling

Hug your knees with your arms, and roll backward & forward. It is good for chronic dyspepsia, constipation and backbone correction.

Hug your knees and roll backward and forward.

Do each exercises many times until your body is relaxed thoroughly.

\<Danjeon Breathing\>

There are three ways of Danjeon Breathing, **lying down**, **sitting** and **moving**.

Sitting Danjeon Breathing is general, so I will explain this.

1. After relaxing the body by doing **Ki exercise**, sit on a chair comfortable.

2. Straighten your back, and put your both hands gently on the knees. Your body is relaxed and very comfortable.

3. Close the eyes gently, and does deep breath 3 - 4 times.

4. Breathe in slowly, counting numbers from 1 to 10 in mind.

5. Breathe out slowly, counting numbers from 1 to 10 in mind.

Breathing must be doing very slowly. When you put a feather in front of the nostrils, it must not move while you are breathing. Focus on counting numbers and breathing. Think nothing.

Imagine that you breathe out carbon dioxide and push **Ki** down to Danjeon during exhalation. Abandon all distracting thoughts and focus to accumulate **Ki** at Danjeon, counting numbers.

6. Does Danjeon breathing for 10 minutes at the beginning.
   Extend your Danjeon breathing time as you become accustomed to it.

7. Breathe deeply 3 - 4 times, and open your eyes gently.

It is important that you have the Very-Silent-Your-Time two times a day when nobody disturbs you, in the morning and the evening, for an effective Danjeon Breathing.

After you are accustomed to Danjeon Breathing counting numbers, you can get a meditation instead of counting numbers. I'm sure you can treat the mental disorders just through Danjeon Breathing.

If you exercise Danjeon breathing for a long time, you can have the ability to feel and use **Ki** through the next steps, **Ki experience** and **Practical use of Ki**.

122

Ki experience

You are able to feel Ki. Don't forget that everyday **Ki exercise** is important. If you do it only whenever you remember, you'd better do nothing. After you accumulate **Ki** in Danjeon through Danjeon Breathing, you can feel the existence of **Ki**. This is the pre-step of **Practical use of Ki.**

Danjeon Breathing is one of **Ki** practices, and there are various kinds of principles in **Ki** practices you must keep in mind. Among them, there is the most important one that you have to remember, **"There is Ki in the place that the mind goes."**

Ki that gathers in Danjeon can be sent to the place that your mind wants it to send through Kyung Rak. After training Danjeon Breathing for about 2 months, you can experience the existence of **Ki**.

Let's feel **Ki** now.

1. Keep the position after taking **Ki exercise,** and start Danjeon Breathing.

2. Spread out your hands, and put them together lightly in front of the chest.

3. Send **Ki,** which is at Danjeon, to the palms. (Your mind lets **Ki** move where you want to send)

Ki is gathering to the palms.

4. When **Ki** gathers in your palms, the palms begin to warm. And **Ki,** that is radiated from the palms, begins to push out the hands.

5. If your both hands become wider in some degree, try to push your hands inside lightly at the same time. You can feel **Something** between your palms, and it rebounds the hands out. It is the same feeling as you push the balloon between your hands.

6. Repeat the above action several times, and feel **Something** between the palms. The **Something** is **Ki**.

7. Gather **Ki** to Danjeon again. Your hands are getting together in front of your chest.

Ki is gathering to Danjeon again.

8. Put your hands lightly on the knees.

9. Do deep breath 3 - 4 times, and open your eyes gently.

Practical use of Ki

You can use your Ki for yourself and others, such as mental treatments, body treatments and so on. During Danjeon Breathing, you sometimes could have an experience that you see yourself sitting and practicing on a chair. To be able to see yourself from outside of your body in spite of your eyes closed, it will be very marvelous for you. This is the moment that you experience the separation of the body and the spirit.

Your spirit is the owner of your body, and it can command your body whatever it wants. Sometimes your body rejects what the spirit commands. It is because the spirit belongs to the Universe (Heaven) and the body belongs to the earth. Your mind is what your spirit thinks.

Now you can send Ki to the place where you want and take advantage of it.

Let's have one example.

When you have a serious headache because of the complicated thoughts,

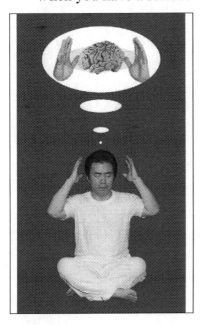

1. Take Danjeon Breathing.

2. Raise your hands to the both side of your head.

3. Imagine your tainted and wounded brain in front of the eyes.

4. Send Ki of Danjeon to the brain.

Polish and treat the dirty and wounded brain cleanly with Ki. The dirty and injured brain becomes clearly and healthfully again.

Your headache will disappear.

Take a deep breath 3 - 4 times, and open your eyes gently. Repeat the above mentioned process until you can feel the effect.

Through such method, you can treat your painful mind and body, and the chronic diseases clearly. First of all, it is important that you believe the principle certainly **"There is Ki in the place that the mind goes"**.

Let's have another example. You can treat your stomachache at the same method.

   1. Put your hands on your stomach, and imagine your painful stomach.

   2. Send Ki of Danjeon to your hands.

Imagine that Ki of your hands cures your stomach, and it'll be getting better.

   3. You can feel your palms are warming.

   4. Polish and treat the dirty and wounded stomach cleanly with Ki.

Your stomachache will feel better.

Korean mothers have been using this treatment whenever her children have a stomachache, from long time ago.

I have explained about the most basic Mental Self-Defense Technique to protect your mental health through Danjeon Breathing so far. The study and practice about Ki is endless because the sphere is so wide and profound. What I introduce here are the most basic ones, therefore the person who is interested in Ki will have to push on in practice still more.

AUTHOR'S NOTE

I wrote about a very small part of the Self-Defense Techniques just like an essay so far. First of all, thank you, all the readers, for enjoying this book all the way through. And thank all the people who helped me to write this book very much, especially Master Ho Yeon Nam, Master Byong Mun Choi, Professor Carl Jorgen Saxer and sincere friend Daniel. I dedicate this book to all of them and grandmaster Nam Jai Kim.

In my point of view, there is no special self-defense technique. As I said before in this book, easy and simple techniques are more powerful and effective than any other complicated ones. Remember and practice the techniques in this book. I am sure you can defend yourself from any dangerous situations by using these techniques.

There are great many techniques in martial arts, and they are changing endlessly. I am studying and training the techniques, and it will continue during my life. I hope you enjoy training martial arts and find sound satisfaction in it.

Master Choi

Master Nam

Thank you again, Master Choi and Master Nam, for helping me while writing this book.

Master Dennis Kim